EDUCATION LIBRARY SERVICE

Browning Way
Woodford Park Industrial Estate
Winsford
Cheshire CW7 2JN

Phone: 01606 592551/557126
Fax: 01606 861412
www.cheshire.gov.uk/els/home.htm

CHESHIRE
COUNTY COUNCIL

Material Matters

Acids & Bases

Carol Baldwin

Raintree

www.raintreepublishers.co.uk
Visit our website to find out more information about **Raintree** books.

To order:
☎ Phone 44 (0) 1865 888113
▤ Send a fax to 44 (0) 1865 314091
▣ Visit the Raintree Bookshop at **www.raintreepublishers.co.uk** to browse our catalogue and order online.

First published in Great Britain by
Raintree Publishers, Halley Court, Jordan Hill, Oxford
OX2 8EJ, part of Harcourt Education Ltd.
Raintree is a registered trademark of Harcourt
Education Ltd.

Editorial: Charlotte Guillain and Isabel Thomas
Design: Michelle Lisseter and Bridge Creative
Services Ltd
Picture Research: Maria Joannou and Alison Prior
Production: Jonathan Smith
Originated by Dot Gradations
Printed and bound in China and Hong Kong by South
China Printing Company

ISBN 1 844 43193 2
08 07 06 05 04
10 9 8 7 6 5 4 3 2 1

British Library Cataloguing in Publication Data
Baldwin, Carol
Acids and bases – (Material matters)
1. Acids – juvenile literature 2. Bases – (Chemistry) –
Juvenile literature
546.2'4

A full catalogue record for this book is available from
the British Library.

Photo acknowledgements
14–15, Andrew Lambert; 18–19, Art Directors & Trip;
13, Art Directors & Trip/A Lambert; 16 bott, Art
Directors & Trip/G Hopkinson; 37 left, Art Directors &
Trip/H Rogers; 12–13, Art Directors & Trip/R Chester;
30, Aspect/K Naylor; 40, Camera Press; 5 top, Camera
Press/F Callanan; 7, Camera Press/F Callanan; 41,
Camera Press/R Stonehouse; 19, Corbis; 24, Corbis; 31,
Corbis; 34–35, Corbis; 40–41, all Corbis; 10–11,
Corbis/A Nogues; 39, Corbis/G Diebold; 9,
Corbis/Hulton Deutsch; 22–23, Corbis/K Fleming; 29,
Corbis/W Blake; 16 right, Farmers weekly; 17 left,
Farmers weekly /; 32–33, Farmers weekly; 28–29,
FLPA/B Borrell Casals; 4–5, FLPA/L West; 43, FLPA/L
West; 18, FLPA/R Tidman; 20–21, FLPA/S Jonasson;
42–43, FLPA/W Wisniewski; 27, Mary Evans Picture
Library; 20, NASA/; 4, Oxford Scientific Films; 40–41,
Photodisc; 16 left, Popperfoto/ Reuters/ Juergen
Schwartz; 15, Robert Harding Picture Library
30–31, Robert Harding Picture Library/K Sherman; 5
bott, Robert harding/K Sherman; 22, Science Photo
Library; 23, Science Photo Library/; 24–25, Science
Photo Library/; 25, Science Photo Library; 26–27,
Science Photo Library/; 35, Science Photo Library/ 36,
Science Photo Library; 38–39, Science Photo Library/;
10, Science Photo Library/ Andrew Lambert; 16 top,
Science Photo Library/ Garry Watson; 42, Science Photo
Library/ Josh Sher; 28, Shot in the Dark Cave
Photography; 6, Trevor Clifford; 6–7, Trevor Clifford;
8, Trevor Clifford; 11, /Trevor Clifford; 12, Trevor
Clifford; 26, Trevor Clifford; 33, Trevor Clifford; 34,
/Trevor Clifford; 37 right, /Trevor Clifford; 38, Trevor
Clifford; 5 mid, /Tudor Photography; 8–9, /Tudor
Photography; 14, Tudor Photography; 17 right, Tudor
Photography

Cover photograph of Linoleic acid crystals under a
microscope reproduced with permission of Science
Photo Library/ EYE OF SCIENCE

Every effort has been made to contact copyright holders
of any material reproduced in this book.
Any omissions will be rectified in subsequent printings if
notice is given to the publishers.

Contents

Any words appearing in the text in bold, **like this**, are explained in the Glossary. You can also look out for them in the Word bank at the bottom of each page.

Outdoor attack

Stinging nettle

Tiny **barbs** on the leaves and stems of stinging nettles can cause painful stings when they rub against your skin. One of the chemicals that causes the pain is **formic acid**. The same acid is also found in the venom of stinging ants.

Something buzzes past your head in the park. You swat at it. Ouch! You have just been stung by a bee. Or was it a wasp? Does it matter which insect stung you? Only if you want to make the pain in your hand go away faster.

Easing a painful sting

When a bee or wasp stings you, it injects **venom**. Bee and wasp venom contain different **chemicals**, so the stings need to be treated differently. Because bee venom is an **acid,** baking soda can help make the pain go away. Baking soda is a **base**. A base is a chemical that can cancel out an acid. Wasp venom is also a base. Treating this sting with vinegar can ease the pain, because vinegar is an acid. It cancels out the base.

Go to page 39 to find out why these treatments work.

The chemical in a nettle sting is acid. Dock leaves can help with the pain because they are **basic**.

Word bank   acid   compound that contains hydrogen and has a pH less than 7
base   compound that feels slippery and has a pH more than 7

Acids and bases everywhere

In nature, acids and bases can be found in places you might not expect. **Citric acid** is what makes a lemon taste sour. Vinegar in salad dressing contains **acetic acid**. Some kinds of tree bark have tannic acid in them. If you have ever got soap in your mouth, you will know it tastes bitter. That is because soap is a base. Baking soda, or bicarbonate of soda, is another base you might have in your home. These acids and bases are not dangerous, but many others are. Some can burn your skin or eat holes in your clothing. They can also clean out that nasty blockage in your drain.

Picking flowers can sometimes end up being a painful experience.

Find out later...

What do acids have to do with sore muscles?

Why does water in a swimming pool need to be tested?

Why are these trees dying?

basic   containing a base
venom   poison injected by stinging or biting

5

Acids and bases

Storing acidic foods

Besides having a sour taste, acids also react with certain metals. For this reason, **acidic** foods like pickles or tomatoes should not be stored in aluminium foil. The acids can eat holes in the foil. Acidic foods like pickled gherkins should be stored in glass or plastic.

Foods are **preserved** in weak acids to stop **bacteria** growing.

Properties of acids

All acids share certain features, or **properties**. The word acid comes from the Latin word *acidus*, which means sour. Acids taste sour. So foods like yogurt, sour cream and pickles have a sour taste. So do grapefruit and tomatoes. But it is definitely not safe to identify acids by taste. Other acids include the liquid inside a car battery. This is very **toxic**.

Acids **react** with certain **chemicals** to produce changes in colour. These colour changes can be used to help identify acids. The chemicals that change colour are called **indicators**.

Fast fact
Acids dissolved in water will conduct electricity.

Word bank   acidic   containing an acid
indicator   substance that changes colour in acids or bases

Common acids

Acids are found in many items people use every day:

- vinegar contains **acetic acid**
- citrus fruits, tomatoes and other vegetables contain ascorbic acid (vitamin C)
- eyewash solutions contain boric acid
- carbonated drinks contain carbonic acid
- sour milk contains lactic acid
- apples contain malic acid
- grapes contain tartaric acid
- your stomach contains hydrochloric acid
- aspirin contains acetylsalicylic acid.

Citrus fruits are just a few of the foods that contain acids.

Muscle acids

When a person exercises, their muscles need more oxygen than usual. The muscles get this extra oxygen by breaking down food stored in their cells. This **chemical reaction** produces lactic acid. If too much lactic acid builds up, a person's muscles will ache.

property feature of something
toxic poisonous

Properties of bases

Bases taste bitter. Soap and milk of magnesia are bases and they have a bitter taste. Drain cleaner and oven cleaner are also bases. But it is definitely not safe to identify bases by taste. Bases such as detergents feel slippery. But strong bases can burn the skin, so touch should never be used to test for bases. Any metal oxide or metal hydroxide is a base. Pure bases are usually solids.

If a base will **dissolve** in water, it is also called an **alkali**. Alkali **solutions** can conduct electricity. Bases **react** with certain **chemicals**, called **indicators**, to produce changes in colour. These colour changes can be used to help identify bases.

Slippery soap

Have you ever dropped a bar of wet soap in the shower? Sometimes soap is so slippery that it just shoots right out of your hand. That is because soap is a base. One property of bases is that they feel slippery.

You can check the labels on household products to find out which ones contain bases. ⟶

Word bank   alkali   base that will dissolve in water
antacid   medicine used to treat upset stomachs

Bases around us

Bases are not as well known as acids. But some common household products contain bases:

- **antacids** used for upset stomachs contain aluminium hydroxide
- deodorants also contain aluminium hydroxide
- building materials like mortar and plaster contain calcium hydroxide
- a solution of calcium hydroxide in water is called **limewater**. It is used to test for carbon dioxide gas. If a person breathes out through a straw into limewater, the limewater turns cloudy white as it reacts with the carbon dioxide
- some antacids contain magnesium hydroxide.

Few foods contain bases. However, egg whites, cooked corn, digestive biscuits, cooked lobster and shrimp and baking soda are **basic**. Other bases, called **organic** bases, are used to make dyes, medicines and clothing fibres.

Lime

Calcium oxide and calcium hydroxide are also called **lime**. When water is added to calcium oxide, calcium hydroxide forms. Both these chemicals can destroy flesh.

During the heavy bombing of London in World War II, lime pits were dug for mass burials of victims of the bombings. This helped prevent the spread of disease.

> > > > > > > >

Turn to page 39 to find out how antacids work.

lime   calcium oxide or calcium hydroxide
limewater   solution of calcium hydroxide in water

Ammonia fountain

The ammonia in the top flask dissolves in water pushed up through a tube from the bottom flask. This reduces the pressure in the top flask and keeps pulling more water up into it, creating a fountain. Universal **indicator** has been added to show the change from **neutral** water to alkaline ammonia solution.

What causes the properties of acids and bases?

Acids are a group of **compounds** that contain hydrogen. When an acid **dissolves** in water, it splits apart and some of the hydrogen is released.

Most bases are hydroxide compounds. When they dissolve in water, they split apart and some of the hydroxide is released. The special **properties** of acids and bases are due to the presence of the free hydrogen and hydroxide **ions** they contain.

Ammonia gas, NH_3, is not a hydroxide but it **reacts** with water. One of the hydrogen atoms from each water **molecule** joins with the ammonia. This reaction produces an alkaline **solution** called ammonia solution, which is sometimes called ammonium hydroxide. It is a base.

Ask your teacher to set up an ammonia fountain in class.

ion   atom or group of atoms with an electric charge
wet cell   battery contaning a liquid that conducts electricity

Acids and bases conduct electricity

Any substance that separates into ions in water can conduct electricity. The human body is about 70 per cent water. There are many substances dissolved in this water. So the human body will conduct electricity. That is why it is never safe to use electrical appliances with wet hands. Since both acids and bases separate in water, they also conduct electricity.

Some batteries are **wet cells**. They contain two connected plates made of different metals or metal compounds. The metals are placed in a solution. Most car batteries contain a series of six wet cells. The plates are made of lead and lead dioxide. The solution is sulphuric acid. Electricity is conducted through the acid.

Lemon battery

A small, safe amount of electricity can be made from a lemon battery. The reading on the meter shows that electricity is flowing. This happens because a **chemical reaction** takes place between the metal wires and the acid in the juice of the lemon.

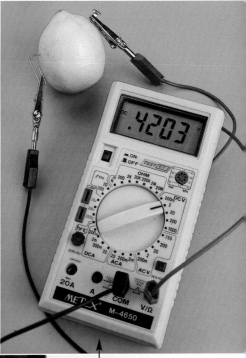

Most car batteries contain sulphuric acid. It can burn skin and eat holes in clothing. So people must be careful when they throw away old car batteries. Acid could splash on them and cause serious injury.

In a lemon battery, the lemon juice conducts electricity.

11

Indicators and pH

Litmus colours

Litmus also comes in liquid form. Here is an easy way to remember the colour that litmus turns in acids and bases:

- An **aciD** will turn litmus **reD**.
- A **basE** will turn litmus **bluE**.

In each case, both words end in the same letter.

Litmus solution turns purple when added to a neutral substance.

Scientists use the **pH scale** to show if something is acidic or basic. The pH scale goes from 0 to 14. If a substance has a pH of less than 7, it is an acid. A substance with a pH greater than 7 is a base. A substance with a pH of 7 is **neutral**. A neutral substance is neither **acidic** nor **basic**.

Indicators

An **indicator** is a substance that changes colour with a change in pH. Indicators change colour at certain pH numbers. They are used to find out whether a **solution** is an acid, a base or neutral.

Litmus

Litmus paper is one indicator that can be used to test for an acid or base. Blue litmus paper turns red in an acidic solution. Red litmus paper turns blue in a basic solution. A neutral solution will not change the colour of either paper. Litmus paper can only show if a solution is an acid or a base, not the exact pH.

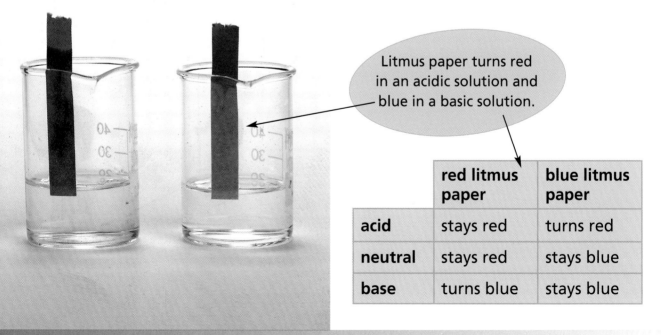

Litmus paper turns red in an acidic solution and blue in a basic solution.

	red litmus paper	blue litmus paper
acid	stays red	turns red
neutral	stays red	stays blue
base	turns blue	stays blue

　neutral　neither acidic nor basic, with a pH of 7

Other indicators

Phenolphthalein (pronounced feen-ul-THAYL-een) is a liquid indicator. It is colourless in an acidic solution. But it turns bright pink in a basic solution. It can only show if a solution is an acid or a base, not how strong it is.

Other indicators tell us more about pH:

- Methyl orange can identify a strong acid. It changes from red to orange between pH 3.2 and 4.4
- Bromothymol blue is a liquid that is yellow below pH 6 and green between pH 6 and 7. It changes to blue at a pH above 7. This indicator can tell you the difference between an acid and a base. But it does not help tell a weak base from a strong base because it is blue in both
- Alazarin yellow is a liquid that is yellow below pH 10, orange between pH 10 and 12, and red above pH 12. It can tell you the difference between a strong base and a weak base.

pH meters

A pH meter can be used to measure the pH of a solution. Two parts of the meter are placed in the solution. The pH reading appears on the dial. Small, battery-operated pH meters can be used by scientists outdoors. Most of them show numbers like those on a digital clock.

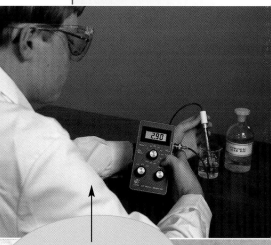

A pH meter is used to give an accurate pH reading.

Water in lakes and streams should be close to neutral. Scientists often check its pH to find out if it has been **polluted** by **chemicals**.

pH scale numbers from 0 to 14 used to indicate the strengths of acids and bases

13

Swimming pool chemistry

The chlorine **compound** used to treat swimming pools is an acid. If the water gets too acidic, it stings your eyes. Swimming pool test kits allow people to check the pH of the pool water. The water should have a pH of about 7.5.

Universal indicator

Universal indicator is a special **indicator**. It comes in paper or liquid form. It is made of a mixture of indicators so it will change colour over the entire pH scale. It does not just show if a **solution** is **acidic, basic** or **neutral**. It also shows how strong a solution is. When a strip of universal indicator paper is dipped in a solution, it changes colour. The package has a **colour chart** on it. By matching the colour of the paper with the colour on the chart, you can work out the pH number.

Adding a few drops of universal indicator solution to a substance shows its pH. The colours of universal indicator are the same as the colours of the rainbow: red, orange, yellow, green, blue, indigo and violet. Strong acids turn universal indicator red and strong bases turn it blue.

The pH of swimming pool water is checked every day.

Turn to page 17 for more swimming pool chemistry.

0   1   2   3   4   5   6

colour chart   chart of colours on universal indicator package that shows the pH of a solution

Natural indicators

Many common materials act as indicators. Tea is a natural indicator. Adding an acid like lemon juice turns tea pale yellow. Adding a base like sodium bicarbonate turns tea dark brown. Try it yourself.

Other natural indicators include the skins of red onions, peaches and apples. Juice from cherries, blueberries or red cabbages is also a natural indicator. Red cabbage juice is bluish-purple, but turns red in a strong acid and violet in a weak acid. It turns greenish in a weak base and yellow in a strong base. It does not change colour in a neutral liquid.

Hydrangeas act as a natural indicator as they grow.

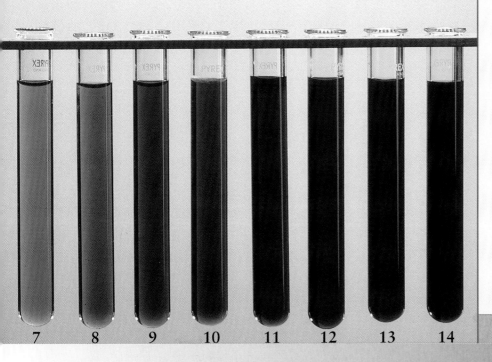

| 7 | 8 | 9 | 10 | 11 | 12 | 13 | 14 |

Flower power

Hydrangeas like these contain a natural indicator. From it you can tell whether the soil in which the flowers are growing is acidic or basic. The flowers will be blue in acid soil and pink in basic soil. They are the only plants that act as indicators while growing.

Snowblowers to the rescue

In 1983, a train ran off the tracks in Colorado in the USA. A tanker wagon overturned and spilled thousands of litres of nitric acid. Firefighters used **snowblowers** to blow powdered sodium carbonate over the spill. The weak base neutralized the acid and no one was badly hurt.

Neutralization reactions

The **chemical reaction** between an acid and a base is called a **neutralization** reaction. In neutralization, both the acid and base lose their **properties**. The **solution** becomes **neutral**. It has neither acid nor base properties.

Most crops grow best in soil with a pH between 5 and 7. Farmers and gardeners often test the pH of their soil. If their soil is too **acidic**, they can neutralize it. They can spread calcium hydroxide, also called **lime**, on their fields or gardens. This base neutralizes the acid in the soil. It does not matter which acids are in the soil or what base farmers use. The products of a neutralization reaction are always water and a **salt**.

acid + base → water + salt

Vegetables grow best in soil with a pH of about 6.5. So farmers often use lime to neutralize acids in the soil.

Acid spills or fires can be very dangerous. Fire crews may blow a base over the acid to neutralize it.

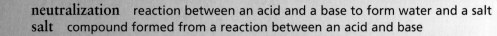

neutralization   reaction between an acid and a base to form water and a salt
salt   compound formed from a reaction between an acid and base

Water and salts

Hydrochloric acid, HCl, is a strong acid. Sodium hydroxide, NaOH, is a strong base. When they react with each other, the hydrogen from the acid and the hydroxide from the base combine. They form water, or H_2O. The sodium and chlorine join to form a salt, sodium chloride. We know sodium chloride as common table salt. But it is not the only salt. A salt is any **compound**, other than water, formed from a neutralization reaction. The metal from the base gives a salt the first part of its name. The non-metal from the acid forms the second part.

Acid	Base	Salt formed
Hydrochloric acid (hydrogen chloride, HCl)	Magnesium hydroxide $Mg(OH)_2$	Magnesium chloride $MgCl_2$
Nitric acid (hydrogen nitrate, HNO_3)	Sodium hydroxide NaOH	Sodium nitrate $NaNO_3$
Sulphuric acid (hydrogen sulphate, H_2SO_4)	Calcium hydroxide $Ca(OH)_2$	Calcium sulphate $CaSO_4$

This table shows the salt formed when each acid and base pair react.

Preventing bacteria from growing in swimming pools takes careful control of the pH.

More swimming pool chemistry

When the pH of the water in a swimming pool falls below 7.4, sodium carbonate, a weak base, is added. It neutralizes the acid and raises the pH. But if the pH goes above 7.6, there will not be enough acid to kill **bacteria** in the water.

Sodium chloride, or table salt, was once as valuable as gold. In ancient Rome, soldiers were paid with it. The soldiers' allowance of salt was called their *salarium*. That is where the English word salary comes from.

Much of the salt we use comes from sea water. The water **evaporates** and leaves the salt behind. It is collected at special salt works.

More about salts

Salts are among the most important **chemicals** in the world. Sodium chloride has thousands of uses. Only a small amount of it is used as table salt. Farmers, meatpackers and makers of food products also use sodium chloride. Farmers use salt for a cattle lick. Meat packers use salt to **preserve** meats. Salt is also used in making glass, treating leather and making other chemicals.

Other salts are also important. Potassium nitrate is used in making fertilizers and explosives. Ammonium chloride is used in batteries. Silver bromide is used to make film for cameras. Sodium bicarbonate is used in baking powder and in making glass. Many products around the home contain salts. They include washing powder, toothpaste and deodorant.

Old books are restored using a weak base to neutralize the acid in the paper. Some chemical remains on the book pages. This helps to protect them for many more years.

brittle   firm, but easily broken
evaporate   change from a liquid to a gas

Saving old books

Libraries around the world have the same problem. Many of the pages in their old books are **brittle** and crumbling away. The pages crack when folded. Libraries want to save their old books, so many are using a chemical process to **neutralize** the acid in the paper. This process uses **vats** of a liquid that contains a weak base. Books are placed in the vat so the liquid can reach all the pages. After about 25 minutes, the liquid is sucked out of the vat. In two hours the books are dry. This process adds hundreds of years to the useful life of the paper.

Fast fact
Since the 1970s, books in the USA, the UK and many other countries have been printed on acid-free paper.

Saving important documents
Some of the first books to be saved are the ones about a country's early history. Machinery for treating items larger than books is also being used. This allows other historic documents, including newspapers, maps and posters to be saved.

Historic documents like this map of the stars may be lost if acid in the paper is not neutralized.

>>>>>>>>>
Turn to page 25 to find out why books become acidic.

More about acids

Acids on other planets

The **atmosphere** of the planet Venus is mostly carbon dioxide gas. But between 40 and 55 kilometres (25 and 35 miles) above the planet's surface there is a thick layer of clouds. The clouds are made of tiny droplets of sulphuric acid.

Sulphuric acid

Sulphur is a yellow solid often found near volcanoes. About 90 per cent of all sulphur produced in the world is burned to form sulphur dioxide gas. This sulphur dioxide is used to make sulphuric acid. Pure sulphuric acid is a colourless, oily liquid. It is used to make fertilizers. Many plants need phosphate fertilizers to grow well. Sulphuric acid is used to break down rock containing phosphate into cheap fertilizer. Sulphuric acid is also used to make clothing, **dyes** and materials like **rayon**. It is used in car batteries and to treat paper as it is being made.

Some **bacteria** on the Earth are able to live in **acidic** conditions. So scientists think we should look for life in the acid clouds of Venus.

Word bank   atmosphere   layer of gases that surrounds a planet
compound   substance made of two or more elements joined together

Properties of sulphuric acid

Sulphuric acid can remove water from many **compounds**. This reaction produces a lot of heat. Because sulphuric acid removes water, it is called a **dehydrating agent**. It causes painful burns because it dehydrates skin. Sugar is a compound of carbon, hydrogen and oxygen. When sulphuric acid is poured on to sugar, the sugar starts to foam and steam. All the hydrogen and oxygen is removed from the sugar. The hydrogen and oxygen form water, which **evaporates** in the heat. Only a black lump of carbon is left behind.

Key to chart
- fertilizer (61%)
- chemicals (19%)
- other industries (7%)
- paints (6%)
- rayon and film (3%)
- petroleum (2%)
- iron and steel (2%)

Volcanoes produce large amounts of sulphur dioxide gas, which **dissolves** in water to form sulphuric acid. The Rio Vinagre is a river in a volcanic area of Colombia in South America. Because of the volcanoes the river water contains weak sulphuric acid. Its water is as acidic as vinegar. That is how the river got its name.

dehydrating agent   chemical that removes water from another substance in a chemical reaction

Royal water

Acids do not usually **react** with the metal gold. However, a mixture of nitric acid and hydrochloric acid is strong enough to react with gold. This mixture is known as *aqua regia*, which means royal water.

Aqua regia was first used to separate silver from gold when the two metals were found together. The aqua regia would dissolve the gold, leaving the silver behind.

Phosphoric acid

Phosphoric acid is another acid that is important in industry. Most phosphoric acid is used to make fertilizers. It is also used to make phosphates. Phosphates are sometimes added to laundry detergents to help them clean better. However, phosphates can cause **pollution** in streams and lakes. They make plants like algae grow very fast. As the algae die, they are broken down by **bacteria**. The bacteria use up most of the oxygen in the water, so fish and other animals die.

Nitric acid

Nitric acid is another acid used to make fertilizers. It is also used to make dynamite and other explosives. In addition, nitric acid is used in plastics such as nylon and polyurethane. Nylon is used in jackets and parachutes. Polyurethane is used in cushions and outdoor furniture.

Fast fact

A small amount of phosphoric acid is added to many soft drinks. It gives drinks a slightly sour but nice taste.

pickling   cleaning the surface of a metal by dipping it in acid
indigestion   upset stomach caused by too much acid

Hydrochloric acid

Hydrochloric acid forms when hydrogen chloride gas **dissolves** in water. Large amounts of the acid are used by the steel industry. **Pickling** is a process that cleans the surface of iron or steel. During pickling, the metal is dipped in hydrochloric acid. Hydrochloric acid is also used to clean stone buildings and swimming pools.

Hydrochloric acid is found in our stomachs. It helps break down foods such as meats, fish and eggs. **Carbonated drinks** contain a weak acid. If we drink too many carbonated drinks, this acid plus the hydrochloric acid already in the stomach can make the stomach too **acidic**. This causes **indigestion**.

Turn to page 40 to read about a different kind of pickling.

◄ ◄ ◄ ◄ ◄ ◄ ◄ ◄ ◄ ◄ ◄
Turn back to page 17 to recall how hydrochloric acid is **neutralized**.

Fizzing rocks

Scientists who study rocks sometimes use hydrochloric acid. Some rocks contain chemicals called **carbonates**. Limestone, marble and chalk are all carbonate rocks. They give off bubbles of carbon dioxide when a few drops of the acid are added to them.

Explosives used in mining and tunnel building are made from nitric acid.

When limestone is dropped in acid it reacts like this. Testing with hydrochloric acid helps scientists identify rocks containing carbonates.

Etching glass

People can write or make an image on glass by using an acid. This process is called **etching**. First, melted wax is used to coat the glass. Next, a design or picture is drawn in the wax with a sharp needle. The needle must go all the way through the wax. The glass is then dipped into hydrofluoric acid for a few minutes. The acid eats into the glass where the needle scratched away the wax. Then the glass is taken from the acid and washed with water. Finally the wax is removed and the design can be seen on the glass.

These glass laboratory objects have been etched using acid.

Glass can be 'frosted' by dipping it in hydrofluoric acid

etching   picture or design made when an acid eats into glass or metal
lignin   gummy substance that binds plant fibres together

Old newspapers and books

Paper is made from plant fibres, usually wood. Wood chips are treated with **chemicals** to break down their fibres. This process makes **wood pulp** very **acidic**. Paper made from wood pulp is also high in **lignin**. Lignin gives trees their strength and stiffness. The lignin in wood pulp also breaks down over time and becomes acidic.

Newspaper is very high in lignin. So it quickly turns yellow and brittle. The pages of many books also turn yellow and brittle after a time. How long a book lasts depends on how acidic the paper is. If the paper is very acidic then it will break down more quickly. Some kinds of paper are made from wood pulp with most of the lignin removed. These papers will last a longer time without yellowing.

◀ ◀ ◀ ◀ ◀ ◀ ◀ ◀ ◀
Turn back to page 19 to recall how old books can be saved.

LIME WATER

Spray away

Formic acid is made in the bodies of ants. They use the acid to bite and sting, but some ants do not even need to do this. They can spray the acid at animals that bother them. People first produced formic acid by crushing ants. An ant hill is also called a formicary.

When an enemy comes too close, this red wood ant sprays acid from its body.

wood pulp   ground-up wood mixed with chemicals; used to make paper

Magnesium sulphate

Magnesium sulphate is found in a product called Epsom salts. Epsom salts are used to help heal certain kinds of skin rash. They were named after Epsom, England, where the salt was discovered in a spring. They have been used since the 17th century.

Acids and metals

Acids **react** with some metals, such as calcium, aluminium and zinc. But acids do not react with other metals such as platinum and silver. A **salt** and hydrogen gas are produced when an acid reacts with a metal. The metal **dissolves** during the reaction and fizzing occurs as hydrogen gas is produced.

For example, hydrochloric acid reacts with the metal sodium. Hydrogen gas and the salt sodium chloride are produced. Sulphuric acid and magnesium react to produce hydrogen gas and magnesium sulphate. Nitric acid and zinc react to produce hydrogen gas and zinc nitrate. Reacting acids with metals is one way that salts can be made in industry.

EPSOM SALTS B.P.
(Magnesium Sulphate B.P.)

Epsom salts, like all salts, are the product of a reaction between an acid and a base. They work by drawing out **organic** waste material from beneath the skin.

crystal   solid in which particles are in an orderly, repeating pattern

Making etchings

Printmakers have used acids and metal plates to make **etchings** for hundreds of years. They use either nitric acid or hydrochloric acid. They also use copper, zinc or iron plates. The metal plate is coated with a thin layer of wax. The artist draws in the wax so parts of the metal plate are uncovered. The plate is dipped in acid. The acid eats away the metal wherever the wax was scratched away. Then the plate is washed and the rest of the wax is removed. The plate is inked with a roller that forces ink into the etched areas. Then the surface is wiped clean. Paper is laid on the inked surface and pressed. The ink from the plate is transferred to the paper, which is now called an etching.

Wide or thin lines

Printmakers use different acids to make thicker or thinner lines on metal plates. Nitric acid is used to make thicker lines. Hydrochloric acid eats deeper into the metal plates. This makes the lines thinner.

Fast fact

You cannot make sodium chloride by mixing sodium and hydrochloric acid together – the reaction would be too violent. Instead you can mix the base sodium hydroxide and hydrochloric acid.

This photo shows a magnified salt **crystal**.

Many great artists have made etchings. They can be very complex.

organic   part of a plant or animal, or made from a plant or animal

Lechuguilla Cave

Lechuguilla Cave in New Mexico formed when hydrogen sulphide gas seeped up through deep cracks in the Earth. The hydrogen sulphide combined with oxygen in underground water to form sulphuric acid. This acid ate through the layers of limestone underground.

Acids and carbonates

Acids **react** with **carbonates** to produce a **salt**, water and carbon dioxide gas. For example, hydrochloric acid reacts with calcium carbonate to form the salt calcium chloride, water and carbon dioxide. Caves form when acids **dissolved** in water reacts with carbonate rocks.

How caves form

The formation of caves starts with rain. Rain water joins with carbon dioxide gas in the air. This forms a weak **solution** of carbonic acid. The acid seeps through cracks in the ground and reacts with calcium carbonate rock like limestone. This reaction dissolves the limestone and forms calcium bicarbonate, water and carbon dioxide. Caves and tunnels form as the acid moves through the rock. After thousands of years, underground rooms and chambers are formed.

stalactite

The effect of acid on Lechuguilla Cave has made it a popular place to explore.

carbonate   compound containing a metal plus carbon and oxygen
draperies   cave formations that hang in folds

Cave features

Water in an open cave loses carbon dioxide into the air. This is like a glass of soft drink going flat. As the water loses carbon dioxide, it becomes less **acidic**. Then it cannot hold all the calcium bicarbonate. The **chemical reaction** works in reverse. As the less acidic water drips and **evaporates**, it leaves behind deposits of calcium carbonate. When water drips from the ceilings, it can form long, wavy shapes called **draperies**. It can also form **stalactites** that hang down from cave ceilings like icicles. As water drips to the floor, towers called **stalagmites** form. Columns form where stalactites and stalagmites meet.

Most **caverns** include several rooms connected by tunnels. The Big Room is in Carlsbad Caverns, New Mexico. It is as large as 4.5 football fields. Its ceiling is more than 87 metres above the cave floor. That is high enough to hold a 22-storey building.

column

drapery

stalagmite

Acidic water dripping underground created these stalactites and stalagmites over many years.

stalactite   icicle-like formation that hangs from the roof of a cave
stalagmite   cone-shaped formation built up from the floor of a cave

Liming

In Norway and Sweden, **lime** is added to lakes to neutralize the acidic water. Liming costs a lot of money and has to be done often to keep the lakes from turning acid again. But liming keeps the plants and animals in the lakes alive.

Acid rain

Acid rain is caused by the burning of **fossil fuels**. Burning these fuels releases sulphur dioxide and nitrogen oxides into the air. These **chemicals** combine with the **water vapour** in air to form sulphuric acid and nitric acid. These acids then fall to the Earth in rain and snow.

Many parts of North America and Europe have been affected by acid rain. Acid rain **dissolves** marble and limestone in buildings and statues. It also kills some types of tree and runs into lakes. Some lakes are now so **acidic** that nothing can live in them. Acid rain also makes soils acidic, so some plants cannot grow in them.

Borsjan Lake in Norway was once dead. Lime was added to successfully neutralize the water.

Fast facts
- Petrol and diesel are made from the fossil fuel oil.
- Many power plants burn fossil fuels to make electricity.

acid rain   rain containing sulphuric and nitric acid
catalytic converter   device that removes chemicals from exhaust fumes

Reducing acid rain

Finding ways to reduce acid rainfall is not easy. One simple way is to use less fuel. Another way is for power plants to use coal with less sulphur. Some power plants treat coal to remove the sulphur before they burn it. Many factories have added **scrubbers** to their chimneys. Weak bases inside the scrubbers **neutralize** the acids in the smoke from fossil fuels. That way the acids do not get into the air.

Cars and trucks burn petrol or diesel fuel in their engines. This produces nitrogen oxides. **Catalytic converters** are now used to soak up the nitrogen oxides in car exhausts. Driving electric vehicles also helps to reduce acid rain.

What can you do?
Conserving electricity and petrol helps reduce acid rain, so:
- turn off lights, computers and other appliances when you are not using them
- only use electric appliances when you have to
- use public transport, walk or ride a bicycle whenever you can.

When acid rain falls on trees like spruce, their needles turn yellow and fall off. Eventually, the trees die.

It seems strange, but riding a bicycle can help reduce acid rain!

scrubber   device attached to a factory chimney to neutralize acids
water vapour   water in gas form

More about bases

Transporting sodium hydroxide

Sodium hydroxide is a **hazardous** chemical. Tankers carrying it have numbers that identify the cargo. The number lets emergency workers know what they are dealing with in case of an accident, even if they do not speak English.

Sodium hydroxide

Sodium hydroxide, NaOH, is one of the strongest bases. Its common name is **caustic soda**. It is a **corrosive chemical**. That means that as well as attacking metals it can burn or destroy flesh. Contact with caustic soda can cause blindness, serious burns and even death. Many other chemicals catch fire or explode when in contact with sodium hydroxide. Because it breaks down oil and grease, **dilute** sodium hydroxide is used in drain cleaners and oven cleaners. These household products always have labels that warn of their danger.

Sodium hydroxide has many uses in industry. It is used to make other chemicals and in paper making. It is also used to process oil and gas and to make soaps, glass and **rayon**.

The number 1726 identifies the chemical being carried. The sign tells us that it is corrosive and will burn skin.

DANGER
Corrosion risk

Watch out for this sign. It is used in laboratories to warn of the dangers of acids and bases.

caustic soda   common name for sodium hydroxide
corrosive   able to attack and change human tissue, metals and other materials

Ammonia is an important base used in many products. Here, ammonium nitrate is being used to fertilize farm fields.

Smelling salts

Smelling salts are sometimes used to wake up people who have fainted. Smelling salts contain ammonium carbonate, sometimes dissolved in water. This chemical gives off ammonia fumes, which irritate the nose and lungs. This causes the person to breathe faster and wake up.

Ammonia

The most widely used base is ammonia, NH_3. Pure ammonia is a colourless gas with a sharp **odour**. More than just a whiff of this gas can make a person very ill. In fact, it can be deadly. Ammonia gas **dissolves** in water to form ammonia solution. Ammonia solution is a very good cleaning agent. Many products used to clean floors and windows contain ammonia. You can usually tell if a cleaning product contains ammonia by the smell.

Most ammonia is made using the Haber process. This process joins nitrogen and hydrogen to make ammonia. Some ammonia is used to make nitric acid. Ammonia is also used in fertilizers and to make rayon and nylon. Ammonium nitrate, used in fertilizers and explosives, is made by **reacting** ammonia with nitric acid.

---

hazardous dangerous
odour smell

Soap making

In ancient times people made their own soap from animal fats and ashes. They mixed these together in iron kettles over an open fire. Soaps are made by **reacting** fats or oils with a base. Wood ashes contain the base potassium hydroxide. People would save the ashes from their cooking fires all year. Then when animals were killed for meat in autumn, they would use the waste fat to make soap. To make hard soap, **salt** was added. The mixture was then poured into wooden moulds and left to set. Then the bars were taken out of the moulds and allowed to air for several weeks. This was done so any remaining **alkali** would be **neutralized**. Otherwise the soap would burn the skin.

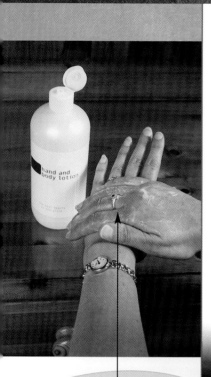

Even a weak base such as soap can harm your skin.

Dry hands

Bases in soap react with oil in your skin, as well as with dirt. Soap can remove too much oil from the skin. The result is dry, rough skin. People like nurses, who have to wash their hands often, use hand lotion to put oils back into their skin.

Fast fact
The word *alkali* comes from the Arabic word meaning 'the ashes', from the ashes of plants.

molecule   group of two or more atoms joined together

How soap works

Soap works by making water wetter than it already is. There is a sort of skin on water called **surface tension**. This has to be broken for something to get wet. Soap **molecules** have two ends. One end of the molecule is attracted to water. The other end is attracted to oil or grease on skin or clothing. The result is that the surface tension of the water is broken. Water can then stick to skin or clothing. As more water is applied, the water-loving part of the molecule pulls the oil-loving end off the skin or clothes, taking the dirt with it. The skin or clothes are left squeaky clean.

Soap scum

Hard water is water that has calcium or magnesium salts dissolved in it. These salts react with soap to form waxy solids called soap scum. Water from areas of limestone rock is often hard.

Today, machines in factories make soap. Once the soap is made, it is washed, dried and formed into bars. Many soaps have perfumes and colouring agents added to them.

Hard water solids get deposited on the sides of bathtubs and on shower doors. They also stick to your skin and hair.

Strength of acids and bases

Tooth decay

Bacteria live in our mouths. When we eat sugary foods, the bacteria get a meal too. The waste products bacteria make from sugars include acids like lactic acid.

These acids are weak acids. But they can still dissolve away minerals in our teeth, causing **cavities**. Saliva is slightly **alkaline**, so chewing sugar-free gum also helps to **neutralize** acids in the mouth.

All acids share certain **properties**. But some acids are safe to swallow, while other acids cause serious burns. So not all acids are alike. Some acids are stronger than others. The same is true for bases.

Sulphuric acid, hydrochloric acid and nitric acid are strong acids. They can cause serious burns. Acetic acid, phosphoric acid, carbonic acid and citric acid are weak acids. These acids are found in foods we eat.

Strong bases include sodium hydroxide, potassium hydroxide and calcium hydroxide. Strong bases are dangerous. Weak bases include ammonium hydroxide, aluminium hydroxide and magnesium hydroxide.

The black part of this X-ray is a cavity caused by weak acids in the mouth. Rinsing your mouth or brushing your teeth after eating a sugary snack will dilute the acid so it causes less damage to your teeth.

cavity   hole in a tooth caused by acids in the mouth
concentrated   having a large amount of a substance dissolved in water

Concentration

Sometimes the strength of an acid or base is confused with its **concentration**. The concentration of an acid or base refers to the amount of the substance **dissolved** in water. A **concentrated** acid has a lot of acid dissolved in the water. A **dilute** acid has only a little acid dissolved in the water.

Lemons taste more sour than oranges do. That is because there is a higher concentration of citric acid in lemon juice than there is in orange juice.

Sometimes drinks are sold in concentrated form. Before you drink them, you have to dilute them by adding water.

Fruit drinks

Some fruit drinks contain 100 per cent juice. Others may contain only 25 or even 10 per cent juice. The rest of the drink is water and sugar syrup. Fruit drinks that contain more juice are more concentrated than those that contain less juice.

If you add a lot of drink concentrate to water, your drink will be concentrated. But if you add only a little concentrate to water, your drink will be dilute.

concentration   amount of a substance dissolved in water

Carbonated drinks

Carbonated drinks contain carbonic acid and sometimes phosphoric acid. But not all carbonated drinks are equally **acidic**. Try using universal indicator and magnesium hydroxide to compare the acidity levels of different soft drinks.

The end point

You can compare the strengths of acids or bases by **neutralizing** them. Place a measured amount of a **dilute** acid, such as hydrochloric acid, in a beaker. Add a few drops of universal **indicator solution**. Then add a base, such as magnesium hydroxide, one drop at a time to the acid and indicator. Count the number of drops added. As soon as the indicator turns yellow, stop adding base. The colour change shows that the base has neutralized the acid. This is called the **end point** of the neutralization reaction. Repeat the experiment with another acid and the same base. The stronger the acid, the more drops of base will be needed to neutralize it.

Bubbles of carbon dioxide are added to drinks to make them fizzy. Some of the carbon dioxide gas dissolves in the drink to form carbonic acid. This makes carbonated drinks bad for teeth.

carbonated drink   drink with carbon dioxide gas bubbles added

An upsetting situation

At some time, most of us have had an upset stomach. Often, the pain is caused by too much acid in our stomach. The extra acid lowers the pH of our stomach contents. **Antacids** are often used to soothe an upset stomach. Antacids contain small amounts of a weak base, such as calcium hydroxide or aluminium hydroxide. These weak bases neutralize the excess hydrochloric acid in the stomach and raise the pH.

If an antacid contains calcium hydroxide, the reaction produces water and calcium chloride.

hydrochloric acid + calcium hydroxide →
water + calcium chloride

If an antacid contains aluminium hydroxide, the reaction produces water and aluminium chloride.

hydrochloric acid + aluminium hydroxide →
water + aluminium chloride

Comparing antacids

You can compare how well different antacids work to neutralize stomach acid. Mix samples of each antacid with equal amounts of water. Then add a few drops of universal indicator to equal amounts of dilute hydrochloric acid. When the **dissolved** antacids are added drop by drop to the hydrochloric acid, the colour change will show you which one neutralizes the acid most quickly.

Baking soda is a weak base. That is why it can be used to neutralize the acid in a bee sting. Vinegar is a weak acid. It can be used to neutralize the base in a wasp sting.

Measuring pH

As well as showing if a substance is **acidic, basic** or **neutral**, the **pH scale** can describe the strength of acids and bases. The lower the pH of an acid, the stronger it is. The higher the pH of a base, the stronger it is. A substance with a pH of 7 is neutral – neither an acid nor a base.

Concentrated solutions of strong acids have a pH near 0. Hydrochloric acid is a strong acid. So, concentrated hydrochloric acid has a pH near 0. Concentrated solutions of weak acids have a pH between 2 and 5. Tomato juice contains citric acid. Citric acid is a weak acid. Tomato juice has a pH of about 4.

Acid can **preserve** food by stopping bacteria from growing.

Safe pickles

People used to make a lot of pickles at home. They needed to be careful when they did this. The pH of dill pickles should be below 3. If the pH is higher, **bacteria** will grow in the pickles, producing the botulinum toxin. This toxin causes a type of food poisoning called botulism.

Word bank preserve stop something from going bad

If you add a little boiling water to very cold water, the water temperature will rise. In a similar way, **diluting** an acid with water will raise its pH slightly. Water is neutral and has a pH of 7. Because this is higher than the pH of the acid, adding water will raise the pH a little.

A concentrated solution of a strong base has a pH near 14. Sodium hydroxide is a strong base. It has a pH of 14. Concentrated solutions of weak bases have a pH range of 9 to 12. Household ammonia is a weak base. It has a pH of about 11. Diluting a base with water will lower its pH slightly.

Some common things have a low pH, while others have a high pH.

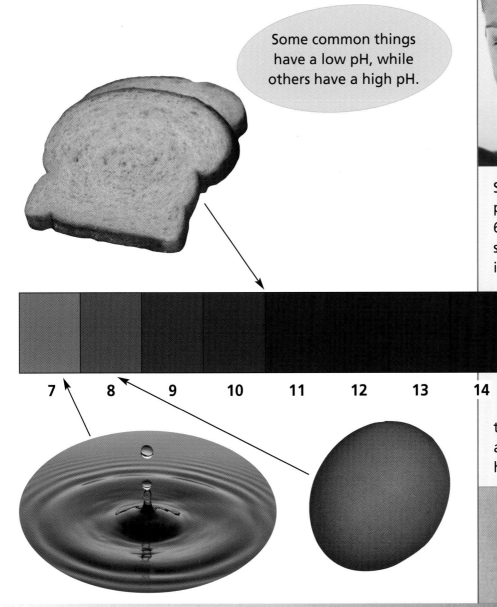

7   8   9   10   11   12   13   14

Skin and hair have a pH of between 5 and 6. A pH-balanced shampoo is one that is close to the pH of our skin and hair. A shampoo that is not pH-balanced can damage hair or make it dull-looking. This is why different types of shampoo are sold for different hair types.

Testing blood pH

Diseases like diabetes and kidney disease can cause low blood pH. Lung diseases like asthma and bronchitis can raise blood pH. People with these problems may need to have the pH of their blood tested from time to time.

Blood in veins contains carbon dioxide, which reacts with the water in blood to form weak carbonic acid. So for a proper test of blood pH, blood must be taken from an artery.

The pH of blood

Blood **circulates** through the body. It carries oxygen to cells and removes carbon dioxide. It also carries food to all body cells. In order for blood to work well, its pH cannot be allowed to change much. **Compounds** called **buffers** allow small amounts of acid or base to enter blood without harmful effects. Buffers help keep blood close to a pH of 7.4 by mopping up these excess acids or bases.

Sometimes, however, blood pH can change too much for buffers to cope. Blood pH that is too high or too low can damage the body's organs, including the kidneys or liver.

Causes of low blood pH:
- drinking poisons such as antifreeze or methanol
- taking too many aspirins at one time.

Causes of high blood pH:
- loss of acid from vomiting a lot
- fast, deep breathing caused by pain
- taking too much bicarbonate of soda for an upset stomach.

Plants like mesquite, aloe, Joshua trees and cacti grow well in basic desert soils.

buffer   acid, base or salt that reacts with added acids or bases to lessen their effects

The pH of soils

Soils can be either **basic** or **acidic**. Acidic soils are found in areas that get a lot of rain. Dead plants rot, or decay, when there is enough moisture in the soil from rain. Decaying plant material is called **humus**. Humus makes soil more acidic. Forests grow in this kind of soil. Evergreens, such as pine and spruce trees, grow best in acidic soil. But if the soil is too acidic, these trees can be damaged.

◀ ◀ ◀ ◀ ◀ ◀ ◀ ◀
Turn back to page 30 to recall how soils can become too acidic.

Minerals that contain calcium and magnesium make soils basic. In some places, these minerals get washed away by rain. In places where very little rain falls, they do not get washed away. There are also few plants to decay and add acids to the soil. Basic soils are usually found in deserts.

Clearing forests for farming

The soil in an evergreen forest is acidic. It may have a pH of less than 4.2. Most food crops grow best in soil with a pH of about 6.5. So, cutting down evergreen forests to grow food is not a good idea.

Blueberries are one of the few food crops that grow well in acidic soil. They can grow in soil with a pH of 4.5 to 5.

circulate   go around
humus   decaying plant material in soil

Find out more

Organizations

The Royal Institute of Great Britain: Inside Out

Science information and resources for young people. Includes quizzes, amazing facts, discussion forums and games.
insideout.rigb.org

New Scientist

Magazine and website with all the latest developments in technology and science. Includes web links for young people.
newscientist.com

BBC Science

News, features and activities on all aspects of science.
bbc.co.uk/science

Books

Chemicals in Action: Acids and Bases, Ann Fullick (Heinemann Library, 2000)

Material Matters: Chemical Reactions, Carol Baldwin (Raintree, 2004)

Materials All Around Us, Robert Snedden (Heinemann Library, 2001)

World Wide Web

If you want to find out more about acids and bases, you can search the Internet using keywords like these:

- 'acid rain'
- acids + bases
- bases + definition
- 'universal indicator'
- neutralization + sting
- 'blood pH'
- acids + KS3

You can also find your own keywords by using headings or words from this book. Use the search tips opposite to help you find the most useful websites.

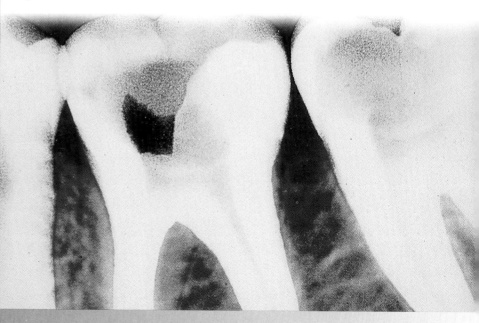

Search tips

There are billions of pages on the Internet so it can be difficult to find exactly what you are looking for. For example, if you just type in 'water' on a search engine like Google, you will get a list of 19 million web pages. These search skills will help you find useful websites more quickly:

- Know exactly what you want to find out about first
- Use simple keywords instead of whole sentences
- Use two to six keywords in a search, putting the most important words first
- Be precise – only use names of people, places or things
- If you want to find words that go together, put quote marks around them, for example 'acid rain' or 'universal indicator'
- Use the advanced section of your search engine
- Use the + sign to add certain words – for example, typing + KS3 into the search box will help you find web pages at the right level.

Where to search

Search engine

A search engine looks through the entire web and lists all the sites that match the words in the search box. It can give thousands of links, but the best matches are at the top of the list, on the first page. Try **bbc.co.uk/search**

Search directory

A search directory is more like a library of websites that have been sorted by a person instead of a computer. You can search by keyword or subject and browse through the different sites in the same way you would look through books on a library shelf. A good example is **yahooligans.com**

Glossary

acetic acid acid found in vinegar

acid compound that contains hydrogen and has a pH of less than 7

acidic containing an acid

acid rain rain containing sulphuric and nitric acid

alkali base that will dissolve in water

antacid medicine used to treat upset stomachs

atmosphere layer of gases that surrounds a planet like the Earth

bacteria living things too small to be seen except with a microscope

barb sharp point that wounds or stings

base compound that feels slippery and has a pH more than 7

basic containing a base

brittle firm, but easily broken

buffer acid, base or salt that reacts with added acids or bases to lessen their effects

carbonate compound containing a metal plus carbon and oxygen

carbonated drink drink with carbon dioxide gas bubbles added

catalytic converter device that removes chemicals from exhaust fumes

caustic soda common name for sodium hydroxide

cavern very large cave

cavity hole in a tooth caused by acids in the mouth

chemical any material made by or used in chemistry

chemical reaction change that produces one or more new substances

circulate go around

citric acid acid found in lemons, limes, oranges and tomatoes

colour chart chart of colours on universal indicator package that shows the pH of a solution

compound substance made of two or more elements joined together; water is a compound of the elements hydrogen and oxygen

concentrated having a large amount of a substance dissolved in water

concentration amount of a substance dissolved in water

corrosive able to attack and change human tissue, metals and other materials

crystal solid in which particles are in an orderly, repeating pattern

dehydrating agent chemical that removes water from another substance in a chemical reaction

dilute having a small amount of a substance dissolved in water

dissolve mix completely and evenly

draperies cave formations that hang in folds

dye colouring material used to colour cloth

end point point at which an acid and a base have reacted completely

etching picture or design made when an acid eats into glass or metal

evaporate change from a liquid to a gas

formic acid acid found in the bodies of ants and in some plants

fossil fuel fuel formed from the remains of plants and animals that lived millions of years ago; coal, oil and gas are fossil fuels

hazardous dangerous

humus decaying plant material in soil

indicator substance that changes colour in acids or bases

indigestion upset stomach caused by too much acid

ion atom or group of atoms with an electric charge

lignin gummy substance that binds plant fibres together

lime calcium oxide or calcium hydroxide

limewater solution of calcium hydroxide in water

molecule group of two or more atoms joined together

neutral neither acidic nor basic, with a pH of 7

neutralization reaction between an acid and a base to form water and a salt

odour smell

organic part of a plant or animal or made from a plant or animal

pH scale numbers from 0 to 14 used to indicate the strengths of acids and bases

pickling cleaning the surface of a metal by dipping it in acid

pollution harmful things in the air, water or land

preserve stop something from going bad

property feature of something

rayon cloth used to make lightweight clothing

react take part in a chemical reaction

salt compound formed from a reaction between an acid and base; sodium chloride is a common salt

scrubber device attached to a factory chimney to neutralize acids

snowblower machine used to blow snow from pavements and driveways

solution solid dissolved in a liquid

stalactite icicle-like formation that hangs from the roof of a cave

stalagmite cone-shaped formation built up from the floor of a cave

surface tension force that pulls molecules of a liquid together at its surface

toxic poisonous

vat large container for liquids

venom poison injected by stinging or biting

water vapour water in gas form

wet cell battery containing a liquid that conducts electricity

wood pulp ground-up wood mixed with chemicals; used to make paper

Index